Then & Now

TONBRIDGE

SALUS POPULI SUPREMA LEX

TONBRIDGE

Then & Now
TONBRIDGE

COMPILED BY PHILLIP BURGESS

TEMPUS

Tempus Publishing Limited
The Mill, Brimscombe Port,
Stroud, Gloucestershire, GL5 2QG

ISBN 0 7524 2099 2

Typesetting and origination by
Tempus Publishing Limited
Printed in Great Britain by
Midway Clark Printing, Wiltshire

The We Three Loggerheads pub used to be the outlet for Bartram's Brewery in the High Street, until it was demolished to make way for the post office in 1900. The pub was well used by the bargees of the River Medway in the nineteenth century. There is still a pub on the site, called the Humphrey Bean. The third loggerhead, of course, is the reader of the sign!

CONTENTS

GENERAL ELECTION 1910.

S. W. DIVISION OF KENT.

TONBRIDGE.

Captain Spender Clay. C. 9240

Alfred Paget Hedges. L. 6020

Conservative Majority 3210

INTRODUCTION

Tonbridge, although often cast in the shadow of its near neighbour, Royal Tunbridge Wells, does in fact hold a trump card over the young upstart – it has more of a history. Tunbridge Wells dates back to 1606, but Tonbridge can boast of a recorded history stretching all the way back to 1066. Although the area has probably been populated since prehistoric times, it was not held together as a cohesive unit until after the invasion of England by William the Conqueror in 1066.

Tonbridge really owes its existence to the River Medway, which splits here into several streams. Five of these streams flow through the town. The River Medway joins the Thames estuary just beyond Garrison Point, Sheerness. Its source is at Turner's Hill, near East Grinstead. It rises, therefore, in Sussex, but it is nevertheless a Kentish river. It divides the Kentish Men, north and west of the Medway, from the Men of Kent, south and east of the river.

Once the castle was built by Richard de Clare, or Richard de Tonbridge, as was the title he took, the town was really on the map. One point of confusion has continued through the ages: how did Tonbridge get its name? Contrary to public opinion, Tonbridge does not mean the 'Town of Bridges'. The more likely answer is that it is derived from the mound or hill-fort upon which the original Saxon keep was built, prior to the present castle. This would have been a 'ton' – a variant of dun or hill – and 'bridge' was probably a corruption of 'burig', or fortress. Until 1870, the town's name was spelt Tunbridge. But, once a 'Local Board District' was established, the spelling was officially changed to Tonbridge to ensure that everybody knew that Tonbridge and Tunbridge Wells were completely different entities.

Tonbridge has many attractions for the visitor. The biggest attraction is the castle. The remains the visitor can see today are those of the castle and gatehouse built in 1260. The castle has 14 acres of grounds, so there is plenty of scope for relaxing walks. The river is also highly recommended, with pleasure boats plying their trade up and down. There are extensive river walks and plenty of fishing opportunities. Tonbridge has many old buildings of which it is rightly proud, from the twelfth-century parish church of St Peter and St Paul, to the fifteenth-century Chequers Inn and the sixteenth-century Ivy Cottage. One of the oldest institutions is Tonbridge School, founded by Sir Andrew Judde in 1553, whose name was also lent to another educational institution in the town, that of the Judd School.

However, Tonbridge offers more than just these attractions. In the past it has been well known as a major printing town and home of cricket ball manufacturers. It is a compact town, with a rich history and something for everyone. It boasts an impressive sports ground, new swimming pool, plenty of historic buildings to catch the eye, and a large number of old pubs and hotels.

Many locals still remember with horror and anger the results of the council's road-widening schemes of the early 1960s, which deprived the town of many of its architectural wonders. The area most affected contained the buildings south of the Chequers Inn, but those buildings left to decay further up the High Street, past the Public Hall near Bordyke, are also worth recalling. Even today, the subject rankles, but we should be thankful that we are at least left with the Chequers Inn and adjoining properties, which could so easily have been added to the scrap heap. The Council of Tonbridge and Malling was granted the privilege of Borough status by Her Majesty Queen Elizabeth II on 19 October 1983. Many new residential estates have been built over the last century, and the town's population now stands at around 30,000.

Regarding the names who have made an impression on the town, we must consider Richard de Tonbridge, who built the original castle, Sir Andrew Judde, responsible for the Tonbridge School, the

Woodgate family, long term owners of Somerhill, Sir Henry d'Avigdor-Goldsmid, who restored Somerhill house to its former glory, Lord de Lisle who inadvertently gave Lucifer Bridge its name, John Hooker, Lord of the Manor of Tonbridge, Captain William Bartram, who gave his name to the brewery, and William Blair, who founded Tonbridge Free Press.

As in my book on Tunbridge Wells, the contemporary photographs in this book are the work of Steven Streeter, whom I again thank wholeheartedly for all his help and eagerness. The after-work shots and long weekends are most appreciated. It was good fun to try and track down certain camera shots, waiting for the right moment, getting out on the river, or just fighting our way through dense undergrowth. I must also thank Jim Angell, for allowing me to delve into his collection of Tonbridge memorabilia. The completion of this book would not have been possible if it were not for his help and advice.

In no particular order, I would also like to thank the following, who have made the compilation of this book that much easier and enjoyable: Mr K.A. Starling, Headmaster of Judd School; Mr A. Nevison; Miss Joy Debney; Mrs Pat O'Brien; Mrs W.M. Carey, Tonbridge Grammar School for Girls; Jim Angell; Iain Fleming, Agent in residence at Fairlawne; Tonbridge School and especially Sue Streeter, for the provision of school photographs; Dawn Foster; Nathalie Andreone; O-Pro Ltd for the use of the Tonbridge Girls' Grammar School hockey team photograph; Ken Passey, Tonbridge Bowling Club; Pat Backhouse, Tonbridge Police Station; Brian Fairweather and children; Phil Higgs, Tonbridge Waterways; Pat Foster, Ryan House; Somerhill School.

Most of the old pictures in this book are from postcards I have collected or borrowed, and date from the early part of the last century. Every effort has been made to obtain copyright permission where necessary. As is usual when researching old information, some names, dates or facts have been muddled or incorrectly recorded over the years. I have tried as far as possible to corroborate these discrepancies with other sources. Please accept my apologies if I have mis-spelt a name or incorrectly noted a date or fact.

BIBLIOGRAPHY

Tales of Old Tonbridge – Frank Chapman
Around Tonbridge – Charlie Bell
Tonbridge Free Press Centenary
Tonbridge School – Septimus Rivington
Mid-Victorian Tonbridge – C.W. Chalklin
Late Victorian & Edwardian Tonbridge – C.W. Chalklin
Tonbridge in the Early Twentieth Century – C.W. Chalklin
Old Tonbridge – Don Skinner
Medway Journey – David J Smith
Bridger's Hand Book of Tonbridge
A Look at the Head and Fifty – Barry Orchard

This drawing from 1735 is entitled 'the south view of Tunbrig-Castle in the County of Kent'. It is one of many illustrations of Kent by Samuel and Nathaniel Buck. This view of the castle depicts the motte (mound) on the left, on top of which are the ruins of the shell keep. The gatehouse of the castle is in the centre, and the parish church is to the right. The column on the far right is the water tower. The River Medway runs along the bottom of the picture and what is now the Big Bridge is just off the picture at the bottom right.

Chapter 1

CASTLE AND

RIVERWALK

Tonbridge Castle. 5.

Pub. by
G. A. Cooper
Maidstone.

The castle from the terrace. The first recorded mention of Tonbridge Castle was in 1066. Richard Fitz Gilbert, who fought with William Duke of Normandy at the Battle of Hastings, was granted the Lowy lands of Tonbridge by the Archbishop of Canterbury, Lanfranc. This was in exchange for his Castle of Brion in Normandy. He then assumed the title Richard de Tonbridge. Tonbridge Castle is also mentioned in the *Domesday Book* of 1086. The castle has had a chequered history; it was destroyed by fire in 1088, only twenty-two years after it was built. In 1260, the stone castle and gatehouse were built. The castle was leased to Thomas Walker around 1644, and most of the buildings were destroyed by Charles I in 1646. It was the scene of many rebellions until 1648; afterwards it was allowed to fall into a state of decay. The ivy shown in the old photograph was removed before the First World War in order to protect the castle.

In 1793 the castle was in the possession of Thomas Hooker, who dismantled the fortifications and reconstructed parts of the building. He started the construction of the mansion house adjoining the castle, but this was completed by William Woodgate of Summerhill, who then gave it to his son as a wedding gift. In 1897 the castle was owned by Lady Stafford, who in 1898 sold it to Tonbridge Urban District Council. Before the sale of the castle to the council, it had been occupied by Dr I.P. Fleming, who used the castle and grounds as a Military Academy for Army students in 1860. When ownership of the castle was passed to the council, it housed a preparatory school for boys. Tonbridge Urban Council took possession of the whole estate in 1900, and they opened the castle grounds to the public on 23 May 1900. Extensive repairs were carried out in 1954, and further work is being carried out in 2000 to enhance access and improve the contents of the guided tour.

The Archway. The north or outer side of the gatehouse is still a striking feature of the castle. Originally, the moat surrounding the castle passed directly in front of it. A moveable bridge was used to cross the moat at this point into what was the central entrance of the castle. This part of the moat was filled in sometime in the eighteenth century, certainly before 1787. The area in front of the gatehouse is now taken over by a small, well-maintained garden and a car park for castle employees. The passageway was well defended, as a door and portcullis were fitted to both ends of it.

The castle from the green, showing the south side of the gatehouse, and the mansion house, which is now home to the Tourist Information Offices. The castle is surrounded by 14 acres of gardens, and has been the most popular tourist attraction in Tonbridge for many years. The castle hosts a varied programme of events, including the May Festival and Carnival, summer band concerts and art exhibitions. It is possible to take a guided tour of the castle, and take in the wonderful view of the town from the top of the gatehouse. In recent years, the castle has become a popular wedding venue, while picnics on the greens have always been a common summertime activity.

The Watergate entrance is situated on the northern side of the Big Bridge, just next to the landing stage where rowing boats are hired out. It provides an entrance onto the Riverwalk, which snakes alongside the river and castle. Unfortunately, the gas lanterns have long since been removed. The trees on the river side of the railings have also been removed, presumably because they were causing a potential danger. The Riverwalk plays host to small fêtes during the summer, normally aimed at families and small children. The ice cream van is almost a permanent feature during the summer months, and one has been happily playing to the captive audience of strollers at the Watergate entrance for many years.

HE NEW WALK, SHOWING CASTLE GROUNDS, TONBRIDGE.

The new Riverwalk was constructed in 1921 to give work to the unemployed of the town. This meant that it was now possible to walk along both sides of the river. The castle remains can clearly be seen to the right of the photographs, high above the river. In the distance is the Boer War Memorial. The Riverwalk is a popular attraction as it soon takes the walker away from the noises and smells of the town centre and into a world of peace and tranquillity. The path on the castle side is popular for pigeon feeding, while the path on the other side of the river passes into the sports ground.

The Memorial pictured here is on the Riverwalk, between the castle walls and the River Medway. It honours the 24 Townsmen and Old Boys of Tonbridge School who gave their lives in the Boer War. It was unveiled on 21 June 1904 by General Sir Redvers Buller VC, DSO, Britain's hero of the war. During the threat of invasion in the Second World War, the memorial was taken down to allow the anti-tank guns a clear line of fire across the Big Bridge. The inscription on the memorial reads: 'Erected by friends to the memory of those whose names are inscribed below, Townsmen of Tonbridge or Old Boys of Tonbridge School who gave their lives in the Boer War to save South Africa for the Empire: 1899-1902.'

RSIDE WALK, TONBRIDGE

The Garden of Remembrance is home to the First World War memorial honouring the 346 local citizens who gave their lives in the war. It was unveiled by General Lord Horne on 24 May 1921. The memorial used to stand in the middle of the road at the junction of Pembury Road and Quarry Hill. However, it was removed after the Second World War. The names recorded on it were included on the memorial erected in the Garden of Remembrance on the Riverwalk, together with those lost in the Second World War and later conflicts. The Garden of Remembrance is situated between the busy High Street and the sports ground, but it retains an air of dignity and peace befitting its solemn purpose.

Chapter 2

THOROUGHFARES

Yardley Park Road, a wide avenue of generous proportions, is situated just off Shipbourne Road on the northern side of the town. It links Shipbourne Road with Hadlow Road. The houses along this road generally date from the turn of the last century or before. However, further down the road, there have been extensive residential developments in the last ten to fifteen years, such as Bickmore Way and The Haydens. At this end of the road, at the junction with Shipbourne Road, the houses have changed very little. The main difference is the establishment of a generous evergreen hedge, presumably to protect the householders from noise pollution and to afford a little privacy.

Yardley Park Rd Tonbridge.

1021. TOP OF QUARRY HILL. TONBRIDGE.

The top of Quarry Hill at the turn of the twentieth century, with very little in the way of traffic. Perhaps the odd horse or cyclist would pass every hour or so. However, with the advent of motor vehicles, the peace and quiet of this tranquil scene would soon be lost. When motor vehicles first came to Tonbridge, Quarry Hill was a popular place to take the cars out for a run. Quarry Hill today is another matter, and cyclists need to take their lives into their hands when attempting to cycle up or down it! It forms part of the busy B2260. The modern photograph is looking up the hill, south towards Tunbridge Wells, and over the A21 flyover which takes traffic down to Hastings or up to London.

Looking down Quarry Hill from approximately the same spot as the previous photograph, it is just possible to make out the spire of St Stephen's church. The cyclists would have a struggle to make it all the way up the hill, which is deceptively steep and long. Quarry Hill is one of two main thoroughfares between Tonbridge and Tunbridge Wells, and a constant stream of cars, buses and lorries make their way up and down the road throughout the day and night. Although a busy road, it is also an extensive residential area, with houses running down both sides of the road. Fortunately, rows of trees still line the road, providing a measure of protection from the traffic noise.

Quarry Hill, Tonbridge.

This view of Brook Street is from Quarry Hill, although when the old photograph was taken it was known as Haysden Lane. This is another road which has changed out of all proportion since the nineteenth century. Although not as busy as Quarry Hill, Brook Street has opened up this southern part of the town. Just around the corner can be found Judd School, West Kent College and Hayesbrook School. There is also a significant residential area further along the road. The early photograph shows a horse-drawn milk cart of the Lodge Oak Dairy, with the horse patiently waiting outside the house on the right, while the milkman makes his delivery.

Looking north towards the High Street from the bottom of Quarry Hill, St Stephen's church spire is clearly visible. To the right is the Foresters Arms pub, which is run by Britain's oldest brewery, Shepherd Neame. Apart from the construction of double lanes to ease the heavy flow of traffic, little has changed between these two photographs. Tonbridge town centre lies just beyond the church and, as can be seen from the contemporary photograph, this is a very busy junction. The double lanes were introduced to allow traffic heading down Quarry Hill to use the right-hand lane to head along Pembury Road, and the left-hand lane to head straight into town. Ninety degrees to the left is the view into Brook Street, shown in the previous pair of photographs.

H ST, TONBRIDGE.

PEMBURY R^D TONBRIDGE, 1051.

A view south-east along Pembury Road at the junction with Quarry Hill. This wide and straight road appears to have changed little over the years, except of course for the ubiquitous heavy traffic. This road is part of the A2014, and as the name suggests, eventually leads to Pembury, several miles out of Tonbridge. On the left the police station, which has just been rebuilt, can be seen. To the right, commercial premises housing a number of small businesses were erected in the 1990s, called Tonbridge Chambers. Pembury Road has helped ease the traffic congestion of the town centre by providing the motorist with a way to bypass the High Street, and leads back onto the A26 towards Maidstone or the A21 towards Pembury and Hastings.

Since the earliest settlements in Tonbridge, the town has had reason to be wary of the River Medway. There have been numerous floods over the years. In 1880 a particularly bad flood hit the town. The area behind the railway station, and especially Danvers Road, was cut off for several days. The residents of this area were passed food in fishing nets. The Bull Hotel in the High Street measured the water level against one of its gateposts at 3 feet. The view in the picture below is from the junction with Barden Road during a flood which occurred on the night of 18/19 November 1911. The last big flood, and probably the worst to hit the town, occurred in 1968. Floods

should now be a thing of the past, thanks to the flood control gates further along the river.

Grammar School, Tonbridge.

At the junction of Bordyke with the High Street, Tonbridge School can be seen on the left. Ferox Hall, another part of the school, is on the extreme right. This junction is heavily used by traffic, with traffic turning into Bordyke heading out along the Hadlow Road towards Maidstone. Proceeding north, London Road leads to Hildenborough. The building to the right of centre in the distance was the Star and Garter pub, but this closed down some years ago and the building is now used as a coffee shop and youth information centre called Switches. It would be extremely dangerous to play in the road today at this point! There is a constant stream of traffic making its way either into or out of the town.

Dry Hill Park Road lies west of Yardley Park Road, just off Shipbourne Road. It is another pleasant residential road, where the church of St Saviour's is found. The spire can be seen in the centre of the photographs. The main building shown is one of two similar buildings adjoining each other. This one is called Dry Hill House, the other Cowdrey House, after Sir Colin Cowdrey, the ex-England cricketer and Old Boy of Tonbridge School. Dry Hill House is one of several registered rest homes in the area. Both houses were built in the 1890s. Cowdrey House was previously used as a residential care home for the elderly, but Tonbridge School purchased this from Tonbridge and Malling Housing Association in 1994. It is now used as a house for day boys of the school.

'Dry Hill Park Rd Tonbridge.1   G A COOPER'S SERIES

Shipbourne Road, Tonbridge.

Looking south towards the junction with Old London Road, at the turn of the twentieth century, there is a row of shops on the left-hand side. The main change to this scene has been the demolition of a row of houses and Mather's greengrocer's shop in the foreground. These were demolished sometime in the 1930s, and when the shop was rebuilt, it was set back some distance from the road. These premises changed hands several times after the Second World War and were later owned by Shipbourne Farm Stores. Now the premises form part of the Unwins Wine Merchants chain. The other shops along this road include a Chinese takeaway, kebab shop and a pub.

Chapter 3

SCHOOLS

Ferox Hall, part of Tunbridge School, situated on the corner of Bordyke and London Road. A house on this site possibly existed as early as the thirteenth century. However, the current property is a sixteenth-century house onto which a Georgian front was added at the beginning of the nineteenth century. It was further altered in 1878/79 and was purchased by a Mr Earl to be used as a boarding house in 1892. Tonbridge School purchased the property in 1919, and they remain the owners today. It has had many distinguished occupants over the years, including several generations of one of the oldest families in Tonbridge, the Children family. During their occupation of the building, between 1750 and 1816, they often entertained Sir Humphrey Davy, the famous scientist, who assisted George Children with his experiments in such subjects as batteries and gunpowder.

The School, Tonbridge

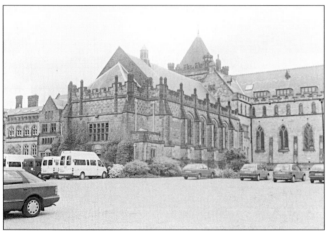

The idea of a grammar school for Tonbridge started in 1525, when Cardinal Wolsey's Commission proposed to set up a 'Free Grammar School for forty scholars, with leaving exhibitions for Oxford.' Unfortunately, the Cardinal fell from popularity and died before the scheme could be carried out. In 1553, Sir Andrew Judde, former Lord Mayor of London and Master of the Skinners' Company, was granted a charter for the foundation of a school at Tonbridge. A stone bearing this date can be found above the headmaster's front door today. The first Headmaster was the Revd John Proctor MA, who remained in charge until 1558, and was probably chosen by Sir Andrew Judde himself. When Judde died in 1558, the administration of the school was left in trust to the Skinners' Company. In 1765, an agreement was established whereby residents of Tonbridge were given the right to send their children to the school. With the introduction of both the railway and a new headmaster, James Welldon, the school experienced much growth in the nineteenth century.

The rear of Tonbridge School. In 1864, the bulk of the old Tudor school was knocked down and replaced by a new structure 60 yards further back, in the Victorian Gothic style, except for part of the headmaster's house. A small chapel was built in 1859, and later used as a library. The school continued to grow during this time, and the number of pupils had risen to 240 by 1875. Further additions were made later that century. In 1887, the Art School and Science Buildings were erected, and in 1894 the clock tower and several extensions were added. Part of the school is a Georgian house known as Old Judde. Originally a private house, it was bought by the school in 1826 for the use of the second master. It is now used for classrooms.

Tonbridge School

The school's front. The iron railings in front of the school were removed in 1940 to help with the war effort. In 1953 Her Majesty Queen Elizabeth the Queen Mother attended the School's 400th anniversary, performing the opening ceremony of a new wall and entrance. The twin boars' heads at the entrance of the school are the symbol of the Skinners' Company. They were carved by Stanley and Leonard Spickett, stonemasons from nearby Lyons Crescent. The school now occupies an extensive site of about 150 acres, and has approximately 700 pupils aged between thirteen and eighteen. About 420 of these are boarders, and 280 are day boys. The school is an integral part of Tonbridge, and it has a reputation for excellence in both the academic and sporting fields.

Kilmarnock, now known as Ravenswood, is one of many off-site properties belonging to Tonbridge School in the north end of Tonbridge. This impressive four-storey building lies just back from the road, shielded by a dense cover of trees. It is situated on the junction of the High Street with London Road. This particular building has changed little over the years, and has been in the hands of the school for some time. Since the time when the school purchased this property, it has been solely used as accommodation for masters of the school. It is in a convenient location and within a stone's throw of the main school buildings.

In 1909, the foundation stone was laid down for Tonbridge School's sanatorium, just off Shipbourne Road. The honour of performing the ceremony went to the Archbishop of Canterbury, Dr Davidson, and two former headmasters of Tonbridge School, Messrs Wood and Tancock. Building commenced immediately, and by 1910 it was completed, at a cost of £10,500. The sanatorium was opened without the usual ceremony due to the death of King Edward VII. It was originally built to accommodate thirty-four patients, and was furnished with the most up to date equipment available at that time. In 1930, the sanatorium matron, Miss Phillips, died from pneumonia, brought on, it was said, by the exhaustion of caring for her patients. That Easter term, the school had been particularly badly hit by a series of epidemics. Under Headmaster Christopher Everett, the sanatorium was sold off in the late 1980s and a smaller one established at the school. The old sanatorium is now known as Ryan House, and is used as a care home.

Due to the success of Tonbridge School, it was decided by the Skinners' Company that a further school should be established. Therefore, Judd School was formed as Sir Andrew Judde's Commercial School in a building called Stafford House, on East Street. It opened after the summer holidays, on 17 September 1888. There was no playground as such, except for East Street on to which the main door opened. This caused a number of complaints, as East Street was a busy thoroughfare. At this time, the school accepted boys from the ages of eight to sixteen, at a cost of £6 per annum. The first pupils were acquired from T.E. Grice's little school in Hadlow Road, just around the corner. William Bryant was appointed headmaster with Grice as deputy. The school started with forty pupils, and ended the year with about eighty.

By 1895, the school was so successful it had to look at the prospect of moving to bigger premises. An 8-acre site was secured, and on 27 April 1895 the foundation stone was laid for new buildings on Brook Street. The building tender was won by Messrs Turners of Watford for £8,637. The school moved into the new buildings in 1896. The following years lead to ever-increasing levels of expenditure in running the school, and so in 1919, the Skinners' Company and the Kent Education Committee came to an agreement for the school to become an 'aided school'. As can be seen from the new photograph, the school has greatly increased in size and stature since its humble beginnings, with the construction of many new buildings. The original buildings are still used, and the number of pupils is now approximately 860. This also includes a number of girls in the sixth form.

The Skinners' Company, responsible both for Tonbridge and Judd Schools, was approached in 1901 with the proposal that it should found a secondary school for girls in the town. While it was in agreement with the idea, there was a lack of funds to carry it out further. The Kent Education Committee, acknowledging that there was a need for such a school, established the County School for Girls in the Technical Institute in January 1905. At this time there were only twenty-one pupils. From here, the school moved to 'Brionne', on the Pembury Road. During the period 1911/12, a new school building was constructed in Deakin Leas, and in 1913 it was opened. The school became known as the 'School on the Hill'. Now it is known as the Girls' Grammar School. The ground floor annexe seen on the right of the contemporary photograph was added as a temporary measure in 1919. As can be seen, it is still going strong today.

Somerhill (previously known as Summerhill) was built around 1611 by the Earl of Glanrickard on the site of an earlier mansion. Later it was given to the Earl of Essex and then to John Bradshaw. The property was restored to the Glanrickard family, and later bought by Thomas Deakin, on whose death it was acquired in 1712 by John Woodgate. Mr Woodgate spent large sums of money on its restoration, and when he died in 1728, thirteen successive members of his family lived on the estate until 1816. At that time, Somerhill was bought by James Alexander. Purchased by Isaac Lyon Goldsmid in 1849, it remained in his family until it was sold in 1981, following the death of Sir Henry d'Avigdor Goldsmid. The house as present-day Tonbridge knows it owes most to Sir Julian Goldsmid. Somerhill is now run as a public school, known as Schools at Somerhill.

The New Council School, now known as the Slade School, is situated in The Slade, just behind the castle. The primary school opened on the 1 February 1907, and the first Headmaster was the well-known local personality Mr G.F. (Gaffer) Stacey. The first pupils to move in were the 320 boys and their teachers from the Bank Street School. The school contained a large assembly hall for drill and gymnastics. It also had seven classrooms with blackboards fitted to the wall, and an asphalt playground. While these might sound like everyday items now, at the time these were quite innovative and cutting-edge. The Master had telephone communications with each room and an electric 'buzzer'.

New Council School, Tonbridge.

Yardley Court was a picturesque building serving as a preparatory school for boys. It was situated in Yardley Park Road, at the northern end of the town. It was founded by Mr A.L. Bickmore MA in 1898. The school was conducted by the same family for many years, but was demolished in the 1980s to make way for extensive residential development. A number of houses now sit on the site of the school, in a close called Bickmore Way. However, this was not the end of the school, for it continues to exist in another form at the Somerhill estate, in the south eastern corner of the town. Here it is one of the 'Schools at Somerhill'.

Tonbridge Swimming Pool was opened in 1910 by Herbert Spender-Clay MP. Even though it was an outdoor pool, it was very popular. The Water Gala of 1914 seen here involves a young boy attempting to walk along a wet pole, at the encouragement of all around. Controversy descended upon the swimming pool in July 1920, when mixed-sex swimming was finally allowed. This episode caused quite an uproar in the local press. However, at this time, mixed-sex swimming was only allowed on Sunday mornings, between six and ten o'clock. The swimming pool closed in 1993 for rebuilding. It finally re-opened as an indoor and outdoor pool on 29 March

Chapter 4
AT WORK
AND PLAY

1996. The opening ceremony was carried out by the Mayor of the Borough of Tonbridge and Malling, Cllr Mrs Pat Barnes, in the company of Duncan Goodhew MBE.

Water Gala. June 1914.

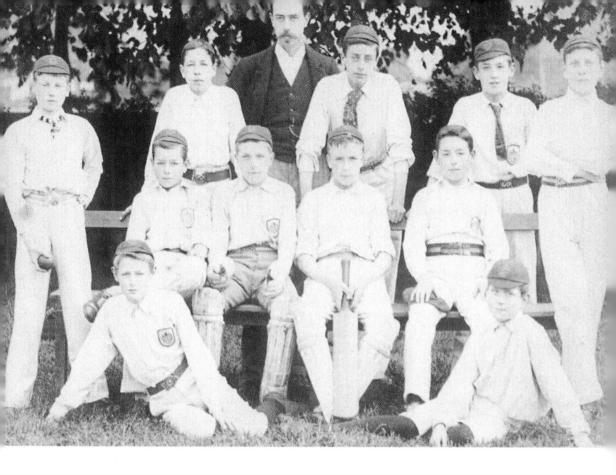

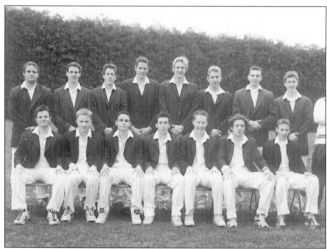

These photographs are of the Judd School's cricket First XIs from 1892 and 2000 respectively. Judd School has a fine reputation for its cricket teams, and it is still a popular sport at the school today. The team today doesn't have to wear the caps and ties that their predecessors did, but the whites are still obligatory and blazers are worn for team photographs. The contemporary photograph does at first glance appear more formal, but at least today's team is allowed to smile. The equipment used is still the same, except that the quality has obviously improved over the century. The cricket balls used by the 1892 team could well have been made in the town.

In 1826, the Governors of Tonbridge School purchased the field which now contains the First XI cricket ground, and the patches of ground to the north and south of it. These were later called the Head, the Upper Hundred and Lower Hundred respectively. The names for these pitches were derived from the numbers of the various games organized by the boys of the school. The First XI ground was originally called the 'Head Eleven' or 'Head Club'. It was later shortened to the 'Head', and that is now how it is universally known. In 1838, the headmaster, Thomas Knox, had the foresight to level the Head by using earth and labour from the new railway workings. The magnificent result was that the Head instantly became a focal point of the school. One famous cricketing journalist is said to have

remarked that the Head was one of the two flattest pitches in the South. Although the pitch received such praise, there were mutterings about the cost of maintaining the grass in tip top condition, and that perhaps the money could be better spent.

In order to enhance the cricketing facilities at Tonbridge School, it was decided to erect a cricket pavilion. The pavilion is situated just off the Head, the pitch for the First XI. It was built in 1860 at a cost of £370, under the superintendence of Mr J.F. Wadmore. Mr Wadmore, an Old Tonbridgian, was always a friend to the school's interests, and was also the architect of the 1859 Chapel. The pavilion was enlarged in 1891 and is now a much cherished and popular haven for the home and visiting cricket teams. From here, there is a wonderful view across the Head, with the picturesque backdrop of the whole school, including the rebuilt chapel.

The Bull Hotel (on the right in the old view) was demolished in 1962 to make way for a supermarket. The site has also been occupied by a Marley DIY store and is now Peacocks, a clothing store. On the extreme left was the Baptist church, which has also now been demolished. On the site now stands the Somerfield store and Woolwich Building Society. As in most High Streets, traffic congestion can be a real problem in Tonbridge. In the days when a farmer could herd his goats through the centre of town, there was probably only a horse or two to worry about. Nowadays, the only time the roads and pavements are almost as empty as they were a hundred years ago is on Sundays, once the market has ceased trading for the day.

High Street, Tonbridge   69979

The coming of the railway to Tonbridge in 1842 opened up a whole new era for the town. Over the last 150 years increased emphasis has been placed on the railway. Railways were laid towards Tunbridge Wells within three years and the line to Sevenoaks followed later that century. There have been rare incidents over the years, such as the collision just outside the town in 1909 when two fatalities were recorded, but without the railway, Tonbridge would not have been able to expand. The days of the steam train, when trains such as the Golden Arrow would run through the station, are long gone. Steam gave way to diesel, which gave way to electric. However, the Eurostar does now pass through Tonbridge on its way between Waterloo and Ashford.

Looking down to the High Street from just below the railway station, these two photographs illustrate several changes. Firstly, the formal way of dressing of the past has disappeared. The three-piece suits and flat caps worn by the men, and the hats and formal dresses of the ladies have given way to comfort. Today people dress to be comfortable: short-sleeved T-shirts, jeans, tracksuits, trainers and leggings are very much the norm, especially among the younger generation. The old Ford Model T and other such vehicles have made way for the cars of today. To saunter across the road at his busy junction now would be unthinkable, due to the constant stream of cars, lorries, buses and bikes travelling along the High Street.

The police have had a long history within the town, and the old photograph here shows the Tonbridge Division of the Kent County Constabulary outside their police station in 1912. The officer on the extreme right, wearing the shoulder-belt and sword, is the division's mounted officer. The Tonbridge Police Division at one time covered eighteen parishes, all controlled from the town, and yet it was still recorded that they were officially overstaffed with five constables! While the uniforms remain in force today, the police force has undergone all manner of changes over the last 100 years. The horse has given way to the motor vehicle, high-tech communications mean the police can arrive at any given location within a few minutes, and the whole organization is run as efficiently as any business.

Tonbridge Bowling Club used to stand behind the High Street and the Angel Hotel. It was formed in 1906, as a satellite of the Cricket Club. In the early part of the twentieth century it was home to cricket, tennis and bowls, and has also staged athletics. For a time it was also the headquarters of the town's professional football club. All were soon relocated except the bowls. The first playing president was F.W. Franks. Fifty-two members each paid a subscription of 2s 6d and the first match was on 4 May 1906. The Kent County Bowls Association was formed on 1 March 1911, with Tonbridge Bowling Club being a founding member. In 1936 the club voted against women being members, but changed their minds the following year. However, women have only played competitively since 1974.

After years of discussions with the council, a new ground was obtained at Tonbridge Farm. The club took possession on 18 March 1994 and played their first match against Whitefriars on 18 May. The official opening was by the Mayor, Cllr Terence Barton, on 3 July 1994.

1907-8

Two First XI hockey teams from Tonbridge Girls' Grammar School. The old photograph shows the team of 1907/08 with the headmistress, a Miss Taylor; the contemporary image shows the team of 1999/2000. It is interesting to note the changes to their costumes, equipment and overall style. The starchy blouses and long skirts are replaced by modern sports clothing of polo shirts with insignias and short skirts. Boots are replaced by training shoes, and of course the hockey sticks have moved with the times and are now lightweight with easy-grip handles. The old photograph has a formal style to it, while the new image, although still a team picture, is far more relaxed with the girls smiling.

Tonbridge Castle has always had the lion's share of the town's pigeons! For years, people have thrown their pieces of bread to the pigeons along the Lower Castle Terrace, by the side of the castle. The same is true today. There are particular spots along the walk where the pigeons congregate and families feed them. Many of the pigeons are so used to having people throw them food that they will often take it straight from the hand of the feeder. It doesn't appear to be only children who enjoy the feeding times either. On most days it is possible to spot the older generation taking their place in the feeding time rituals too.

Feeding the Pigeons, Tonbridge Castle.

The landing stage on the River
Medway used to be owned and run
by the Norton brothers, and in
particular Bert Norton, son of Lijah,
who started off in the boat-building
business. At this time, the beginning of
the twentieth century, rowing boats
could be hired for as little as a shilling
an hour. From 1900 until the Second
World War, Venetian fêtes were held on
the river every year, for which boats
were grandly decorated. Bert's brother
Syd, an expert boatbuilder, gained a
reputation for coming up with
beautifully designed entries for the fête.
After the war the fêtes were revived, but
they never attracted their pre-war levels
of enthusiasm. While the rowing boats
remain today, safety concerns must now
be considered. Hence in the
contemporary photograph, the children
in the boat are wearing their safety
jackets. The landing stage is now run by
Tonbridge Waterways, who hire out
various sizes of rowing boat for £7 an
hour. Another modern innovation is
that they can also hire out motor boats
from the landing stage.

Children always have loved swings and they will continue to do so. While there are no longer donkeys to play with, there are still swings for children to use. For safety reasons, modern-day swings are made with metal frames, not relying on the strength of the old wooden-framed contraptions. The swings in the contemporary photograph are situated just behind the castle near to the Slade School. Again, it is interesting to note how clothing has changed over the years. A hundred years ago, it was quite normal for young boys to wear suits and girls to wear bonnets and lace-up boots, although this may well have been their Sunday best. Today, children are more comfortable in tracksuits, trainers and T-shirts. Hats are certainly not worn any more, with the possible exception of a baseball cap.

The once commercially viable river now plays host to a number of pleasure craft. However, along the river are many clues to its past as a commercial waterway, especially the old wharves down from the Big Bridge. The Medway has played an important part in the development of Tonbridge from a small hamlet to an industrialized town. However, boaters have not always enjoyed a peaceful scene such as the one pictured. In the early nineteenth century, there was a long-running dispute with a local landowner, Lord de L'Isle, who objected to boating and skating on a particular stretch of the river at Barden. He put up barriers to keep people away, but the boaters broke them down. Chains were used, but these were cut. One night somebody

Chapter 5
RIVER MEDWAY

wrote on the bridge which linked Barden with the footpaths to Leigh, 'How art thou fallen from heaven, O Lucifer'. The town laughed at this, and Lord de L'Isle allowed access from then on. The name Lucifer Bridge stuck when the old bridge was replaced.

On the Medway, Tonbridge.

This location was locally known as The Point, and is situated just off the sports ground, near Lucifer Bridge. It was a popular place in the past for fishing and swimming. It was a well-known spot to catch large pike, whilst bream and roach were also caught. Fishing took place all along the river with the exception of the Riverwalk and the castle where it was not allowed. While fishing is still allowed, with the appropriate permit, swimming is actively discouraged and considered dangerous. As Tonbridge swimming baths boast four pools, there is no need to swim in the river any more. Today, the only activity around The Point is the odd boat rowing up the river.

Cannon Bridge was originally a footbridge in the Postern Deer Park. This was part of the South Frith area attached to Tonbridge Castle. It used to take Mill Lane over the River Medway, linking the corn mill at the bottom of Mill Lane with the forge and hammer mill at Postern. This was in the seventeenth century, when the property was owned by Sir Peter Vanlore. The bridge was altered many times over the years to allow barge traffic through. It collapsed in 1911 through neglect, and was rebuilt in 1915. It was rebuilt again following the severe flood which hit the town in 1968. Today's bridge is seldom referred to as Cannon Bridge. Mill Lane no longer passes over the river; it has given way to the busy mini by-pass called Cannon Lane.

Cannon Bridge, Tonbridge

were removed and the water course was diverted by the Southern Water Authority, at the time of the construction of Leigh flood relief barrier to alleviate flooding downstream. The flood relief barrier was constructed during 1979/80 and completed in 1981. It was built to prevent any further flooding of Tonbridge, which had been a hazard for centuries; the last major flood had occurred in 1968. It was built across the flood plain of the Medway 3km upstream from Tonbridge. When operated, it diverts excess floodwater over agricultural land upstream of the sluice, reducing the risk of flooding to the town. It has successfully prevented flooding on numerous occasions; typically, it is called into action twice a year.

The Weir is another well-known spot on the river above Tonbridge. It was popular with a number of different people, including campers, swimmers and fishermen, but it has now disappeared. The sluice gates

The water pumping station. A water company was in existence from the early 1850s, when the waterworks were opened. However, very few homes were connected to the mains. All the other homes had to rely on their water from wells, many of which were polluted. There were several campaigns to persuade the local authority to purchase the water company but 'parish pump politics' prevented this and today it forms part of the West Kent Water Company. In May 1911, it was reported at the AGM that they had 176 customers, and were pumping about 2,000 gallons of water per hour. The water was obtained from gravel pits. Today the company, which later amalgamated with Sevenoaks Water Company, has extended its area and supplies water to an ever-increasing population.

782:
TONBRIDGE: THE RIVER.

These views are taken from the river looking back towards the Big Bridge. In the original photograph, the railings of the Lower Castle Terrace can be seen on the left, and to the right is Bridge House and Bartrams Brewery. The house and brewery have long since gone. The contemporary photograph shows the pleasure boat *Caxton,* run by Tonbridge Waterways, which provides one-hour return trips through the town lock and out into the open countryside. The river's traffic has been reduced to predominantly pleasure craft since 1915, when ten new locks and flood control sluices were built. At the Tonbridge lock, hand-operated rack and pinion tumbler sluices are still in use.

The Castle Inn from the riverbank. Midland Bank (now HSBC) was built on the corner after the demolition of Bridge House and Bartrams Brewery, which adjoined it. The council's town improvement scheme lead to its purchase of the brewery and house. The original Castle Inn was built on this site in 1700. In 1871 the local board bought the land on the east side of the bridge, including the Castle Inn, in order to make the bridge bigger. The local brewery sold the land for £1,600. The original bridge was built in 1775. The new bridge, several times larger than the original, was officially opened on 19 September 1888. It has since been known as the Big Bridge. It was built by Wallis & Sons of Maidstone at a cost of £2,146, and used to have gas lanterns running along it. It was not until 1994 that the Big Bridge had to be strengthened to cope with the increased weight of traffic.

ONBRIDGE. CASTLE HOTEL & BRIDGE.

River Medway, Tonbridge

The River Medway was made
navigable as far as Maidstone in the
seventeenth century, and it opened for
traffic at Tonbridge in 1741. The first
barge arrived at the Town Lock from
Maidstone. The locks were suitable for
40-ton barges and so at this time the
river dominated all commercial
transport in the area. Freight carried on
the river included coal, timber, iron,
lime and road-stone. A Medway
Navigation Company was formed in
Tonbridge in 1739, and it set up its
wharves along Medway Wharf Road,
which is where these photographs were
taken. The most important of all the
river-serviced industries were the
Powder Mills at Leigh, with their water
powered machinery and barge-borne
traffic. These wharves played an
important part in Tonbridge life up to
the end of the nineteenth century.
However, the Medway Navigation
Company was beset with litigation
problems, and its decline was
accelerated when it failed to respond
effectively to the competition of the
railway, which arrived in Tonbridge in
1842.

O f the ten locks still in use on the Medway, the highest is at Tonbridge, 60ft above high tide at Allington lock (between Aylesford and Maidstone). Most of the barges worked up to Tonbridge were man-hauled. This meant that progress was painfully slow, and the Medway Navigation Company failed to see the consequences of this. It also neglected its locks. The Upper Medway Conservancy Board took control of the river in 1911 and closed it while the neglected locks were rebuilt. The river officially reopened on 4 August 1915, but by this time, the trade had been lost to the railway. In the 1920s coal was still brought to the gasworks, and as recently as 1950 a tug

towed a 200-ton barge loaded with coal up the river to the gasworks in a futile effort to revive the trade.

48246. TONBRIDGE: THE TOWN LOCK.

The Big Bridge in the centre of these photographs was originally built in 1775, at a cost of £1,100. The design was by Mr Milne and it replaced the existing bridge, which was deemed inadequate for the needs of the town. The Castle Inn, with the pointed roof, cannot be seen in the contemporary photograph because the HSBC bank on the western side of the bridge obscures it. This stretch of the river is very popular with pleasure craft. The canoe club is nearby, and the landing stage where rowing boats and motor boats can be hired is at the Big Bridge. Tonbridge is the official limit of navigation of the River Medway. However, if craft can clear the 6ft 6in headroom offered by the Big Bridge, they may travel a further two miles towards Penshurst.

Boat-building has been carried out on the Medway for years. Makers concentrated mostly on rowing boats and canoes, and the industry went into steep decline after the Second World War. One of most famous boatbuilding names in Tonbridge was Norton. The business was started by Lijah Norton, who passed it on to his sons, Syd and Bert. Syd Norton continued his boat-building business until the 1950s. Bert concentrated more on the rowing boat hire business at the Big Bridge, but of course there was an obvious link between the two. The Nortons also dredged the river bed for gravel for industrial use, along a stretch of the river known as Long Reach.

Looking across the river to Bartrams Brewery and the landing stage. The brewery was owned by W. and G. Bartram Ltd, and was also known as Bridge Brewery; it was demolished along with Bridge House, home to Capt. William Bartram. The brewery used to serve the We Three Loggerheads pub, which was demolished in 1900 to make way for the post office. In place of the brewery and house, the private house pictured was erected, along with the old Midland Bank (now HSBC). The Lower Castle Terrace is on the right between the castle and the river, and the foreground shows the Norton brothers' landing stage for their rowing boat hire business.

The Voluntary Aid Detachment hospital had a short but important part to play in the history of Tonbridge. Situated on Quarry Hill, the hospital was available for the treatment of soldiers in the First World War. Soon after the outbreak of war in August 1914, Tonbridge was preparing itself to accept the war wounded. The first group of men, forty-five in all, arrived at the hospital on 19 October 1914. A war fundraising effort was started in the town to support the injured and this continued up to 1919. The hospital was soon in danger of being overrun, as it had over 500 patients by February 1916. The influx continued unabated, and as late as

early 1918 two marquees had to be erected in the grounds to cater for all the patients. The VAD hospital finally closed in February 1919.

V.A.D. Hospital, Tonbridge.

TONBRIDGE. POST OFFICE & BRIDGE.

The Old Post Office. At an auction of surplus land, William Hodgskin bought a plot of land on the river, opposite the Castle Hotel. He then erected a building, which at that time held one of Tonbridge's few public clocks. The building was leased to the Post Office before their permanent building over the bridge was completed. The new post office building was completed in 1906 on the site of the old We Three Loggerheads pub; it is now the Humphrey Bean pub. Once the Post Office had vacated the building shown here, the building was used by the NatWest Bank for many years Now it is part of the Pizza Express chain. This photograph was taken from the Lower Castle Terrace, adjacent to Water Gate. Also pictured are the Big Bridge and a number of developments along Medway Wharf Road.

The original police station, on Pembury Road near the junction with Quarry Hill, was built in 1864. The buildings consisted of the station itself and a courthouse. Before this was built, prisoners used to be locked up in two 'cages', which were in Bank Street and Barden Road. The police station served its purpose for over 130 years, but late last century it was decided to demolish it, as it was no longer able to keep up with the requirements of the growing police force. The old station was finally demolished in 1996 and its replacement was erected on the same site. It was opened by His Royal Highness the Duke of Kent on 13 May 1998. The new police station is much larger than the previous one, and houses approximately 300 personnel.

of the current shop was a meadow until 1900, when James Harris built Bradford House on the junction of the High Street with Bradford Street. The shop was previously occupied by Harris the drapers before it was taken over by John Angell. Upon John Angell's death in 1973, the business was carried on by two of his sons, John and James. The business expanded to Maidstone in 1926, Dover in 1934, Deal in 1935 and to Folkestone after the Deal shop became a wartime casualty. The Tonbridge branch is now run by David Angell, son of James.

John Angell, the jewellers, was established in 1830, and is therefore one of the oldest businesses in the town. It has been in the same family since 1910, and is still entirely family-owned. Mr Angell took over an established business at 112-114 High Street, and moved to the current premises at 64 High Street in 1960 when the old premises were demolished as part of the council's street improvement scheme. The site

Fairlawne is one of the largest houses of the district. For many years, Fairlawne was home to the Vane family, having been purchased by Sir Henry Vane, grandson of Sir Henry Vane of Hadlow. Sir Henry, a Republican in the time of Charles II, was convicted of high treason and executed on Tower Hill in 1662. His son, Christopher, was created Lord Barnard by William III. He died at Fairlawne in 1723 and was buried in nearby Shipbourne church. His son, also William, succeeded him but died in 1734. The estate passed out of the Vane family on the death of William's son, William Hollis, in 1789. It was bequeathed to David Papillon and later purchased by Mr Yates, a relative of Sir Robert Peel. He died in 1834 and left everything to his daughter. Upon her death, the estate passed to Joseph Ridgway. Later, Fairlawne was home to the Cazalet family for many years. Major Peter Cazalet was the trainer of the Queen Mother's horses, and she was a frequent visitor to Fairlawne at that time.

The Old Ivey Cottage, Tonbr

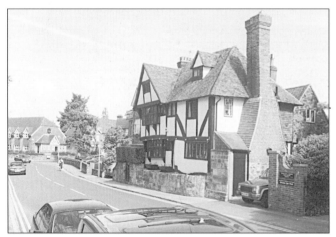

This timber-framed building is known as the Port Reeve's House. There were no brick houses in the town at this time; it was constructed of lath and plaster. It is on the south side of East Street, just off the High Street. It is one of the oldest houses in Tonbridge, known to be over 450 years old. It was formerly known as Old Ivy House or Old Ivey Cottage. Like the Chequers Inn, this is probably one of the most photographed buildings in Tonbridge apart from the Castle. It is uncommon to find a building of such age, and in as good condition as this is, which is still used as a private residence. Even today the house attracts many admirers.

The Port Reeve's House was formerly the home of the Fiscal Officer. This gentleman was responsible for levying a toll on all cattle, sheep and commodities that entered the town by the old Postern Gate, which led onto the meadows to the east of the town. The house was originally two separate dwellings, but it was converted into a single residence when it was then called Port Reeve's House. It is also said to have been the Old Swan Inn at one time, giving its name to Swan Lane. Swan Lane later became East Street. The house has long since been a private residence and due to its enduring popularity, it is hoped that its remarkable state of preservation will continue for another 450 years. The garden of the house contains evidence of the old Fosse, or town ditch, which ran through the area centuries ago.

TONBRIDGE STATION.

The railway arrived in Tonbridge in 1842 from Redhill, and signified the start of a boom period for the town. The original station, built at this time, was at first on the other side of the road. In 1845 a line was established to Tunbridge Wells, but it was not until the line to Sevenoaks was built in 1868 that the station was moved to its current location, on the bridge over the railway, as seen here. The station's façade was altered in 1934. It received another facelift in the 1980s when the present tiling was added. Looking north, in the background St Stephen's church can be seen at the bottom of Quarry Hill.

Tonbridge is in an excellent position to benefit from the railways, and it is because of this that it has flourished in the 150 years since the railway was established. The River Medway, for so long a regular and important source of income, rapidly fell out of favour as a means of transporting raw materials. The railway was a more efficient and quicker means of transport. The population has also expanded because, amongst other things, people moved to the town as commuting to London became straightforward. It takes less than an hour to get to the mainline London stations. Tonbridge has seen the golden era of the steam train, when the stationmaster used to wear a top hat. The modern-day equivalent would be the Eurostar service, which powers through the station daily between Waterloo and Ashford.

This house has changed remarkably little over the years. It is reached by taking the new Riverwalk and heading into the sports ground, which is a private road for vehicles but a public thoroughfare for pedestrians. It is a private residence, built probably around the turn of the nineteenth century or a little before. The personal jetty has now gone because land has been reclaimed from the river. Adjoining this house to the right is Tonbridge canoe club. The origins of the house are unknown, but it is quite possible that it was first constructed with the maintenance of the water pumping station in mind, which is 100yds or so further along the walkway into the sports ground.

The High Street from the northern end looking south towards the Big Bridge. The Chequers Inn can just be made out to the right of centre. On right was Chas Baker and Co. Ltd, motor works. They had car showrooms at 150 High Street. The building on the left with the porch is the Rose and Crown Hotel. The buildings at this end of the town are little changed from a century ago, except perhaps for the shop windows, which now tend to be plate glass. The gentleman cycling through the middle of the road would certainly have a shock today if he tried the same thing. The level of traffic has increased out of all proportion to when this photograph was taken, and so traffic-

calming measures have been implemented. Recently attempts have been made to modernize this part of the town, with the establishment of several new wine bars.

High Street, Tonbridge

For many years, a focal point of the southern end of the town was the Angel Hotel. It was situated on the corner of the High Street and Vale Road, facing the Public Library. The severe floods of 1968 badly affected this area, as was usual whenever a flood occurred. Unfortunately for the Angel Hotel, it was badly damaged at this time and in 1972 it was demolished when the surrounding area was developed. Standing on the site of the old hotel for several years was a branch of Queensway, but now the premises have been occupied since the 1990s by a branch of the Poundstretcher chain. This part of the High Street is very busy, and the roundabout was installed to try to alleviate the congestion which always builds up here.

Tonbridge Library stands on the corner of Avebury Avenue and the High Street. It was built next to the site of the old Toll Gates. These marked the southern boundary of town until the arrival of the railway. The site of the library was formerly occupied by the Temperance Hotel and the shops of G. Terry and J. Lambert. These were all demolished in order to build the library. The Library was built in 1900 as a 'Free Public Library and Technical Institute', at a cost of £7,000. Five years after it was completed, the library played home to Tonbridge Girls' Grammar School, as the school at that time had no permanent premises from which to operate. The library now houses the public lending library and the reference

section, as well as the town's adult education centre. The Station Tavern on the left has recently been converted into a café, called Molly's.

1886, the post office opened from 7 to 9 a.m. on weekdays and 7 to 10 a.m. on Sundays. It had three deliveries a day, except on Sundays when there was just one. The garage in the middle was owned by H.E. Hall & Co., who claimed to be the 'sole county agent for the noiseless Napier cars', as well as for Talbot cars. To its left was J.W. Larby, booksellers.

The Old Post Office ceased to be used for that purpose many years ago. After standing empty for a time, it was purchased by the J.D. Weatherspoon chain of pubs. They reopened the building as a pub in the late 1990s, calling it the Humphrey Bean. Hall's is now empty, and the booksellers' premises now houses two distinct shops, a newsagents and an opticians.

The post office was established on this site during the First World War after moving from its temporary premises just over the Big Bridge. When it was in the temporary premises, in

This building, now the Castle Inn, used also to contain William Blair's printing premises. William Blair was only twenty-three when he founded Tonbridge's first newspaper, in May 1869. He called it the *Tonbridge Free Press*, not because he was giving the newspaper away, but because it was free of any political bias. He first set up his business in the High Street, then expanded into better premises seen here on the corner of Medway Wharf Road. Due to a road-widening programme, he had to leave these premises in 1887 in order for them to be demolished. The Castle Inn was also demolished at this time and later rebuilt in the style which is seen today. William Blair died in 1900 aged fifty-five. His paper continued to run for over 100 years until the competition from its rival, the *Kent and Sussex Courier*, proved too great.

W illiam Rathbone's shop, 112-114 High Street (the watchmakers), was taken over by John Angell in 1910. The two shops were jewellers and haberdashers, run by Mr and Mrs Angell respectively. It started off in the hands of a watchmaker called Asher Barcham in 1830. The buildings were constructed around 1575. On the left is Gunner's the drapers, whose department store lasted until the early 1980s. The demolition of these buildings in 1960 caused uproar in the local and national press. It is a decision that even now provokes intense feelings amongst the people of Tonbridge, who at the time accused the Tonbridge Urban District Council of vandalism. It was claimed that Angell's, which looked as old as the Chequers Inn due to its frontage, had to be demolished because it was in such poor condition. Two Tonbridge councillors admitted this was not the case to Jim Angell once the deed had been done.

The Chequers Inn is probably one of the most photographed buildings in Tonbridge, after the castle. It was built in the late fifteenth century and, with its front-facing gables, is one of the finest examples of a Kentish timber-framed building that can be found today. It has been a focal point of the town on this part of the High Street since it was first erected over 500 years ago. The inn served as a posting house for horse-drawn carriages in years gone by, and today still enjoys the popularity afforded it by its old-world charm and its prime location next to the castle and river. The inn gives some idea of the heritage of this part of the town which was lost during the road-widening programme enforced in the early 1960s.

CHEQUERS INN, TONBRIDGE.

94088

Looking north up the High Street, the old Town Hall stood just below the junction of Castle Street. It was built on the site of the market place and stocks in 1798, and served its purpose for just over 100 years. One of the last functions to be held in the Town Hall was the proclamation of King Edward VII's accession in 1901. The Town Hall was demolished in May 1901 to widen the High Street. Although the town benefited from the extra space, it lost an important part of its heritage in this area of the town. On the left is the shop of Walter Peters, pawnbroker, which immediately adjoined the Chequers Inn on the south side. This shop was occupied by White & Co., ironmongers, prior to demolition.

The Rose and Crown Hotel is another famous Tonbridge landmark. It is a timber-framed coaching inn with an eighteenth-century façade. Its porch stretches out across the pavement and it was traditionally the place from which election results were announced. The coat of arms is of the Duke and Duchess of Kent, parents of Queen Victoria. The Rose and Crown was an important stopping point for the horse-drawn coaches and carriages which travelled from London through Tonbridge and on to the coast in the eighteenth and early nineteenth centuries. Many parts of the hotel still retain their original character, with oak beams and Jacobean panelling. It has forty-nine en-suite bedrooms, a restaurant, lounge, bar, and three function rooms.

The Public Hall, High Street, Tonbridge.

The Public Hall was built in 1873, and opened later that year. It was originally used for theatrical performances and concerts. It has also been used to hold church services. It became the Public Hall Cinema in 1921, and opened with the film *Suds* starring Mary Pickford. The Public Hall never quite won the hearts of the locals like the old Town Hall, and has been struck by misfortune over the years. On Boxing Day 1926 a fire broke out and th hall was forced to close. It re-opened as the Capitol Cinema two years later. It closed again in the late 1960s, only to re open as a bingo hall. Later, it was a snooker hall and also housed a video rental shop. However, it was again hit by a fire in 1997 which destroyed the building, leaving only the empty shell, which remains today.

Following the arrival of the railway at Tonbridge in 1842, and the consequential rapid increase in the population of the south end of the town, there was an urgent need for a new church. An appeal was made for public subscriptions to build the church of St Stephen. It was decided to build the church at the bottom of Quarry Hill. The foundation stone was laid by Lady Hardinge in May 1851. The church was completed the following year and consecrated by the Archbishop of Canterbury on 26 October 1852. The first vicar was Revd C. Dallas Marston. In 1853 a separate parish of St Stephen's was created, with its northern boundary

Chapter 8
CHURCHES

being the stream which flows under the Little Bridge in the High Street. Additions to the church over the years include the north aisle in 1866 and the clock and bells in 1879.

48247 TONBRIDGE: ST. STEPHEN'S CHURCH.

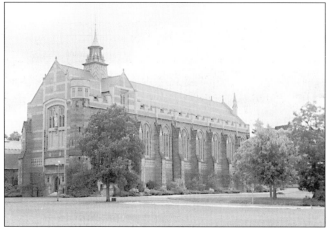

At the end of the nineteenth century, the Charity Commissioners approved the expenditure of £15,000 for Tonbridge School's new chapel. The Decoration Committee, formed in 1896, suggested that the money should be used to build the fabric of the chapel, and that the cost of the interior should borne through subscriptions. The foundation stone was laid on 22 May 1900. The architect was Mr W. Campbell Jones. Local sandstone quarried in Tunbridge Wells was used for the exterior and interior. The internal roof was of pine; externally it was covered in green slates. The Sanctuary was paved with marble. It was built to seat 500.

St Augustine of Canterbury's Chapel was consecrated on 26 May 1902 by the Archbishop of Canterbury, Dr Temple. The west of the chapel was left incomplete until 1909 because of lack of funds. The cost of completion of the fabric of the chapel in 1908/09 was £13,019, making a total cost of £30,847. On 17 September 1988, to the town's horror, fire destroyed the chapel.

When the chapel burned down, the school governors initially intended to build a new chapel, but their proposal was rejected as the school stands within a conservation area. It was therefore decided to rebuild the shell. The architect Donald Buttress, surveyor for Westminster Abbey, was called in to assist. Restoration of the chapel started in October 1992, and it was an enormous undertaking. It was completed in October 1995 at a cost of £7 million. On 20 October 1995, the restored chapel was dedicated by the Bishop of Rochester, Dr Michael Nazir-Ali, before a congregation of 870. One of the focal points of the chapel is the new organ, built by Marcussen & Son of Denmark, widely regarded as one of the finest organ builders in the world.

It took a year to build, and a further six months for installation and voicing (there are 4,830 pipes). The inaugural recital was given to an audience of 700 by Simon Preston on 17 November 1995.

Priory Road   Tonbrid

St Stephen's Mission Hall was built a an expansion of the nearby St Stephen's church in 1880. It stood near the junction of Rose Street and Priory Road. The old view here was taken around 1904 and faces the railway bridge. The Mission Hall was constructed by a local builder, Mr Eason, at a cost of £450; the land was given by the vicar of St Stephen's. The hall consisted of a large room, with a classroom or vestry adjoining it. It had a Gibbs small-pipe heating apparatus. The opening service was conducted by the vicar, Revd R.L. Allnutt, on 13 October 1881. The hall closed some time ago and the building was used commercially by Bramley Services. It is now used by Kentec Tool Hire.

In 1873, residents at the north end of the town were clamouring for a new parish and church, as the existing parish church was becoming overcrowded. To this end, they formed a committee of residents. On October that year they wrote to the Archbishop of Canterbury, Archibald Campbell Tait, detailing the reasons for their request. They also advised the Archbishop that they had been promised land by a Mr George Stenning. It was not until April 1875 that the Archbishop advised the committee that a new parish would not be created. However, he did allow for a new chapel of ease to be built. The foundation stone was laid on 31 July 1875, on a corner plot of Dry Hill Park. The land was given to the committee by Mr John Deacon, a parish patron. The architect was Ewan Christian, and the builders Messrs G. Punnett & Sons. The church, built in the early English style, cost £3,000. Seating for 252 worshippers was provided. St Saviour's church was consecrated by the Archbishop of Canterbury on 15 July 1876.

Looking northwards towards St Stephen's church from the railway station at the corner of Priory Road with Quarry Hill. The old photograph dates from around 1900 and shows Webber's Nursery, which was later Rawson's Garage and Quarry Hill Parade. Mr Webber's shop and glasshouses were on the opposite side of the road. Established in 1882, this business closed in 1963 on Mr Webber's retirement. The Quarry Hill Parade shops include a newsagent, a couple of food establishments and a music store, to name but a few. The building now on the corner plot once occupied by Webber's is a residential care home. The foundation stone was laid on 4 June 1998 by Michael Webber, chairman of Tonbridge and Malling Housing Association.

St Giles' church, Shipbourne, is a completely different style of church to St Stephen's. This church is situated several miles north of Tonbridge, along the Shipbourne Road. It is a very pretty and compact church which completely dominates its small hilltop location overlooking the Green. A chapel stood here in the fifteenth century, at which time it belonged to the Knights Hospitallers of St John. The old chapel was demolished and a new one constructed in 1722 by Christopher Vane of Fairlawne, otherwise known as Lord Barnard. It was designed by James Gibbs, better known as the architect of St Martin-in-the-Fields and St Bartholomew's Hospital in London. When Lord Barnard died in 1723 he was buried at the church.

The church was again rebuilt in 1880/81 by another resident of

Fairlawne, Edward Cazalet. When he died several years later he too was buried at the church.

The interior of the church is also worth a look. It contains many high-quality Victorian carvings, furnishings and decorations. The memorial to the first Lord Barnard can still be seen, having been brought from the earlier church. There are also several mural monuments, the main one being in memory of Edward Cazalet's grandson, also Edward, who perished in the First World War.

Parish Church Tonbridge.

G.A.COOPER'S SERIES

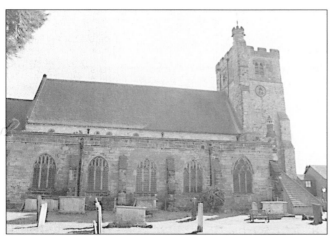

The old parish of Tonbridge was, until the nineteenth century, the largest in Kent. It was approximately 8 miles north to south, and $5\frac{1}{2}$ miles east to west. Originally in the diocese of Rochester, it was transferred to Canterbury in 1846, only to be restored to Rochester again in 1905 as that diocese had been reduced in size by the creation of the diocese of Southwark. An earlier church existed on the site of the parish church of St Peter and St Paul in Saxon times. The first Norman church, built probably in the twelfth century, forms the core of what is now the oldest part of the building. The chancel was rebuilt in the thirteenth century and a nave and tower were erected. During the fourteenth century, the tower was raised and the north aisle added. Much of the external work seen today is from this time. Buttresses were added during the fourteenth century to correct the church's tendency to lean southwards. This view shows the north side of the church, with the earliest of the three nave aisles, the fourteenth-century north aisle.

In 1663, a gallery over the north aisle was erected for the use of the boys of Tonbridge School. This gallery survived for two centuries. The south aisle was also added around this time. The peal of eight bells dates from 1774. The church had been enlarged in 1820, but due to the increased number of worshippers, in 1877 it underwent an extensive restoration and enlargement programme. The last services to be held in the church before the overhaul took place on 29 July 1877. For almost two years, the congregation had to worship over the road in the Public Hall. The church finally reopened on 11 June 1879. The church had undergone numerous alterations, both internally and externally. Firstly, the church was completely re-roofed. The north, south and west galleries and the old box pews were all removed. The nave

5418. Parish Church & Old Cottages, Tonbridge.

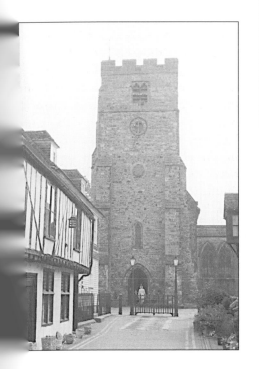

and the south aisle were rebuilt. An additional south aisle was also constructed from local sandstone, to accommodate the boys of Tonbridge school who had formerly used the north gallery. The three-decker pulpit was also replaced and a font was added. This view of the church is from one of the oldest thoroughfares in the town, Church Lane.

The architect for the renovation work of the 1870s was Ewan Christian and the builders were Messrs G. Punnett & Sons. This was the same team responsible for the construction of nearby St Saviour's church in Dry Hill Park Road. The church organ was also rebuilt and enlarged at this time, and this was re-commissioned on 18 December 1879. The full cost of restoring the church and rebuilding the organ was almost £15,000. The church is ever-popular today, and is one of the notable landmarks in Tonbridge. This view of the church is from Church Street, showing a row of old cottages to the left.